FAMILY PASSOVER HAGGADAH

הגדה של פסח

ELIE M. GINDI

COMMENTARY AND FORWARD
RABBI LEE T. BYCEL

EDITOR
PAMELA B. SCHAFF

EMG PUBLISHING
PO Box 49832, Los Angeles, CA 90049
Phone/Fax (310)476-1565

Distributed by
SPI BOOKS
136 W. 22nd St., New York, NY 10011
(212)633-2023 - Fax (212)633-2123

This haggadah is dedicated to

Moses Elie Gindi

who died on the first night of Passover, 1965.

May his memory be a blessing to his children

and to his children's children . . .

Special thanks for their invaluable help:
Carla Barr, Alissa Guttman, Justina Klimkevich, Manya Polonsky

FOREWORD

Pesach is a remarkable holiday. Its main celebration is in the home. The Seder allows us to experience both slavery and freedom, as we tell young people a story that is at once ancient and modern. We eat a wonderful meal, visit with friends and family, discuss contemporary issues, and sing songs. The haggadah is our guide through the Seder. This haggadah was created for Seders that include people of all ages; the story is told in a manner in which children can freely participate. An initial section on preparing for the Seder provides useful hints and ideas for the leader. Text boxes with guiding questions and engaging commentary are scattered throughout, encouraging thoughtful discussion. The description of sources following the text provides informative background regarding each image.

The unique aspect of this haggadah is its tribute to illuminated haggadot throughout the ages. For many centuries, artists have interpreted the Passover story through their creative works. Elie M. Gindi conveys this compelling story with an approachable text and specially selected reproductions of images from these magnificent haggadot, along with captivating pictures of young people enacting parts of the Seder. This radiant and colorful haggadah encourages the participant to experience the Seder not simply through words, but through a feast of rich and vibrant imagery.

My family and I were privileged to be present when this haggadah was first introduced in experimental form. I will never forget the sparkling eyes of the children and adults as they turned from page to page, discovering another print from an illuminated haggadah. This elegant volume invites all participants to experience fully the Pesach story. The captivating pictures, combined with the story rendered in a friendly and readable manner, create a haggadah which will help you teach the mysteries of Pesach while uplifting the spirits of all at the Passover table.

Rabbi Lee T. Bycel
January, 1998

PREPARING FOR THE SEDER

Passover is a family holiday. It's a good idea to read and tell Passover stories to children before the holiday arrives. Encourage children to prepare for the Seder: help them create art objects or Seder plates, have them practice the "Ma Nishtanah," ask them to prepare an answer to a Seder question or help them design a skit or appropriate costume. On the night of the Seder, table activities such as coloring books or paper on the table on which to draw a Passover scene will keep the younger children occupied and interested.

In this haggadah, colorful images surround a concise, readable text, with shaded boxes that include questions, interesting facts or topics for discussion. The leader chooses which boxes to include and sets the pace for the Seder. Important concepts when formulating an overall Seder plan include:

- ◊ Keep within a reasonable time period. The Seder using this haggadah should take approximately 45 minutes before and 15 minutes after the meal, though this may vary depending on the amount of discussion.
- ◊ Gauge the level of discussion to keep the interest of the participants.
- ◊ Decide on a format that will encourage questions and discussion.

The ideal environment is one of comfort (reclining is suggested), where those present freely participate in the reading of the haggadah and in the resulting discussion. The spirit of Passover is to include individuals with whom you might not ordinarily dine, Jews or non-Jews. Those with curiosity about the holiday and its traditions are excellent candidates. It's a mitzvah to invite someone in need.

SEDER CHECKLIST

- ◊ haggadot
- ◊ Seder plate
- ◊ holiday candles
- ◊ cup for Elijah
- ◊ cup, basin and towels for hand washing
- ◊ wine cup for each person
- ◊ small plates for symbolic foods
- ◊ matzah cover or bag
- ◊ pillows for reclining
- ◊ kids' projects, fun items, or props
- ◊ wine
- ◊ matzot: for participants, three to be covered, and an extra "Matzah of Hope"
- ◊ roasted egg for the Seder plate, hard-boiled eggs for participants - "Beitza"
- ◊ parsley or celery for "Karpas"
- ◊ roasted bone (lamb or chicken) - "Zeroah"
- ◊ horseradish, bitter lettuce or bitter vegetable for the bitter herb - "Maror"
- ◊ romaine or other bitter lettuce for "Chazeret"
- ◊ charoset (mixture of apples, nuts, wine, and spices; some use dates, nuts, and wine)
- ◊ salt water for dipping

Searching for chametz - From the *Second Cincinnati Haggadah* - Amsterdam, 1716/17

SEARCHING FOR CHAMETZ

Children often enjoy the ritual of searching for chametz, the term for leavened food (food and drink made from grains such as wheat, barley, rye, oats, or their derivatives). The night before Passover, gather the children with the necessary tools: a candle, feather and spoon. Ahead of time, place some bread around the search area. Turn the lights off and allow the children to find the chametz by candle light. They will scoop up the crumbs by using the feather and spoon.

Recite the following biblical passage and prayer:

> "Remember this day as the day you left Egypt, from the house of slavery. It was with a mighty hand that God led you out. No chametz should be eaten." (Exodus 13:3)

בָּרוּךְ אַתָּה יְיָ אֱלֹהֵינוּ מֶלֶךְ הָעוֹלָם אֲשֶׁר קִדְּשָׁנוּ
בְּמִצְוֹתָיו וְצִוָּנוּ עַל בִּעוּר חָמֵץ.

Ba-ruch a-tah A-do-nai E-lo-hey-nu me-lech ha-o-lam a-sher kid'sha-nu b' mitz-vo-tav v'tzi-va-nu al bi-ur cha-metz.

Blessed are You, Eternal God, Ruler of the Universe, who has sanctified us with laws and commanded us to remove chametz from our homes.

THE SEDER

This book is a haggadah. Haggadah means "the telling." By reading the words of the haggadah we tell the story of Pesach, the Hebrew word for Passover. "Pass over" refers to the tenth plague that befell Egypt and passed over Israelite homes. Our ceremony for Passover is called the Seder, which means "order." Through this traditionally ordered ritual, we will retell the story of the Israelites' journey from slavery in Egypt to freedom in the Promised Land, eat special foods that symbolize Passover's many messages, and teach our children the traditions of Pesach, first celebrated more than 3000 years ago.

Telling the story of Passover is one of the most important mitzvot in Jewish life. The Torah tells us, "You shall tell the Pesach story to your children in the days to come." (Exodus 13.8)

Tonight's Seder is not just the retelling of an ancient and compelling story. Rather, we are asked actually to experience the bitterness of oppression and the sweetness of freedom so we may better understand the hope and courage of all men and women, of all generations, in their quest for liberty, security, and human rights.

An ancient rabbinic text instructs us, "Each person in every generation must regard himself or herself as having been personally freed from Egypt." (Mishnah Pesahim)

We have before us family and friends, a beautifully prepared table, a great feast, and a traditionally arranged Seder plate. Let us recline, enjoy, learn, and relive the dramatic and miraculous Pesach.

? Jews have celebrated Pesach for more than 200 generations. How many generations of people are at your Seder table?

"Ha lachma anya," the traditional first three words of the haggadah, mean: "This is the bread of affliction."

From the *Spanish Haggadah*, 1350-60

CANDLE LIGHTING

Before the Seder begins, we light and bless the festival candles. In Jewish tradition, the day begins and ends at sunset. These candles symbolize the transition to a new day and remind us that Passover is a holy time.

בָּרוּךְ אַתָּה יְיָ אֱלֹהֵינוּ
מֶלֶךְ הָעוֹלָם אֲשֶׁר קִדְּשָׁנוּ
בְּמִצְוֹתָיו וְצִוָּנוּ לְהַדְלִיק נֵר
שֶׁל (שַׁבָּת וְשֶׁל) יוֹם טוֹב.

Ba-ruch a-tah A-do-nai E-lo-hey-nu
me-lech ha-o-lam a-sher kid'sha-nu
b'mitz-vo-tav v'tzi-va-nu l'had-lik ner
shel (Shabbat v'shel) Yom Tov.

Blessed are You, Eternal God, Ruler of the Universe, who has sanctified us with the commandment to light the (Sabbath and) holiday candles.

? How is your Seder table the same or different from the one in this scene?

From *Haggadah for Passover* - 1921

THE ORDER

PARTICIPANT:

There are 14 steps in the order of our Seder.

1. KADESH
קַדֵּשׁ

The blessing

2. URCHATZ
וּרְחַץ

Hand washing

3. KARPAS
כַּרְפַּס

The greens

4. YACHATZ
יַחַץ

Breaking the middle matzah

5. MAGGID
מַגִּיד

Telling the story

6. RACHTZAH
רָחְצָה

Second hand washing

7. MOTZI MATZAH
מוֹצִיא מַצָּה

Blessing for the matzah

14. NIRTZAH
נִרְצָה

Conclusion

13. HALLEL
הַלֵּל

Praising God

12. BARECH
בָּרֵךְ

Blessing after the meal

11. TZAFUN
צָפוּן

The afikomen

10. SHULCHAN ORECH
שֻׁלְחָן עוֹרֵךְ

The meal

9. KORECH
כּוֹרֵךְ

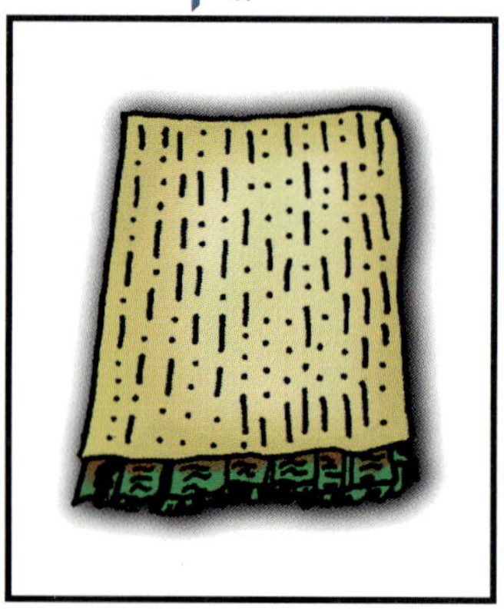

Hillel's sandwich

8. MAROR
מָרוֹר

The bitter herbs

If there are children at your table who made Seder plates or other Seder symbols, now would be a good time for them to share their creative work.

THE SEDER PLATE

PARTICIPANT:

On our table is the Seder plate on which are six symbolic foods.

THE ZEROAH, a roasted shank bone, reminds us of the special lamb that was brought to the Temple in Jerusalem on Passover as an offering to God.

THE BEITZA, a boiled egg, is smooth and round and symbolizes the new life that comes with the spring.

MAROR, a bitter herb, reminds us of the bitterness of Egyptian bondage.

CHAROSET, a mixture of wine, nuts, and pulp, represents the mortar our ancestors used in building the pyramids in Egypt.

KARPAS, a green vegetable, reminds us that Passover occurs during the spring when new life brings a feeling of hope.

Tiered Seder plate - Vienna, 1814

CHAZERET, the bitter herb used in a sandwich, follows the custom established by Hillel, a wise rabbi and teacher, to remind us that our ancestors ate matzah and bitter herbs together.

1. KADESH - The blessing
קַדֵּשׁ

PARTICIPANT:

Wine symbolizes the "joy of life." Tonight we drink wine four times during the Seder, representing God's four promises to the Israelites of redemption from slavery, which are mentioned in the Book of Exodus (Chapter 13):

1. "I will free you."
2. "I will deliver you."
3. "I will redeem you."
4. "I will take you to be my people."

Wine is a symbol of sanctification in Jewish life. In Jewish thought, no object or action is intrinsically good or bad. Its value is in the way it is used or misused.

PARTICIPANT:

With the first cup of wine we recall the first promise found in the Torah, “I am Adonai, and I will free you from slavery in Egypt.”

From *The Haggadah*
Arthur Szyk, 1965

בָּרוּךְ אַתָּה יְיָ אֱלֹהֵינוּ
מֶלֶךְ הָעוֹלָם בּוֹרֵא פְּרִי הַגָּפֶן.

Ba-ruch a-tah A-do-nai E-lo-hey-nu me-lech ha-o-lam bo-rey p'ri ha-ga-fen.

Blessed are You, Eternal God, Ruler of the Universe, who creates the fruit of the vine.

בָּרוּךְ אַתָּה יְיָ אֱלֹהֵינוּ מֶלֶךְ הָעוֹלָם אֲשֶׁר
בָּחַר בָּנוּ מִכָּל עָם וְרוֹמְמָנוּ מִכָּל לָשׁוֹן
וְקִדְּשָׁנוּ בְּמִצְוֹתָיו. וַתִּתֶּן לָנוּ, יְיָ אֱלֹהֵינוּ,
בְּאַהֲבָה [שַׁבָּתוֹת לִמְנוּחָה וּ]מוֹעֲדִים לְשִׂמְחָה,
חַגִּים וּזְמַנִּים לְשָׂשׂוֹן, אֶת יוֹם [הַשַּׁבָּת הַזֶּה,
וְאֶת יוֹם] חַג הַמַּצּוֹת הַזֶּה, זְמַן חֵרוּתֵנוּ,
[בְּאַהֲבָה] מִקְרָא קֹדֶשׁ, זֵכֶר לִיצִיאַת
מִצְרָיִם. כִּי בָנוּ בָחַרְתָּ, וְאוֹתָנוּ קִדַּשְׁתָּ
מִכָּל הָעַמִּים [וְשַׁבָּת] וּמוֹעֲדֵי קָדְשֶׁךָ
[בְּאַהֲבָה וּבְרָצוֹן] בְּשִׂמְחָה וּבְשָׂשׂוֹן
הִנְחַלְתָּנוּ. בָּרוּךְ אַתָּה יְיָ מְקַדֵּשׁ
[הַשַּׁבָּת וְ]יִשְׂרָאֵל וְהַזְּמַנִּים.

(On Sabbath)

Blessed are You, Eternal God, for selecting us as being worthy of Your covenant, and for sanctifying us through Your commandments. In Your love, You have given us (Sabbaths for rest,) festivals for rejoicing, holidays, and seasons of joy, including this festival of Passover, the time of our freedom, the sacred occasion commemorating the Exodus from Egypt. Blessed are You, Eternal God, who sanctifies (the Sabbath,) Your people Israel and the festivals.

SHEHECHEYANU

ALL:

בָּרוּךְ אַתָּה יְיָ אֱלֹהֵינוּ מֶלֶךְ הָעוֹלָם שֶׁהֶחֱיָנוּ
וְקִיְּמָנוּ וְהִגִּיעָנוּ לַזְּמַן הַזֶּה.

Ba-ruch a-tah A-do-nai E-lo-hey-nu me-lech ha-o-lam she-he-che-ya-nu, v'kiy'ma-nu, v'hi-giy-a-nu, laz-man ha-zeh.

Blessed are You, Eternal God, Ruler of the Universe, who has kept us alive and sustained us and allowed us to reach this season.

All drink the first cup of wine while reclining.

2. URCHATZ - Hand washing
וּרְחַץ

LEADER:

We wash our hands as a way of getting ready. During Urchatz we do not say a blessing. We are free to wash, recline, read, remember, learn, and teach.

The leader of the Seder pours water over each hand.

3. KARPAS - The greens
כַּרְפַּס

PARTICIPANT WHO WAS BORN IN SPRINGTIME:

We remember that it was springtime when the Passover story took place. As we dip greens in salt water, we remember the tears of our ancestors who suffered as slaves in Egypt and the tears of those who still are not free today.

SONG OF SONGS 2:10-12

Arise my beloved, my fair one,
And come away;
For lo, the winter is past
Flowers appear on the earth,
The time of singing is here.
The song of the dove
Is heard in our land.

Let us go down to the vineyards
To see if the vines have budded.
There will I give You my love.

From the *First Cincinnati Haggadah*
Southern Germany, c.1480-90

? What signs of springtime have you seen so far this year? What else can you expect?

We dip parsley, celery, or lettuce in salt water and recite the prayer.

ALL:

בָּרוּךְ אַתָּה יְיָ אֱלֹהֵינוּ מֶלֶךְ הָעוֹלָם בּוֹרֵא פְּרִי הָאֲדָמָה.

Ba-ruch a-tah A-do-nai E-lo-hey-nu me-lech ha-o-lam bo-rey p'ri ha-a-da-mah.

Blessed are You, Eternal God, Ruler of the Universe, who creates the fruit of the earth.

4. YACHATZ - Breaking the middle matzah

יַחַץ

Matzah comb
Germany, 18th-19th century

The leader uncovers the three matzot, takes the middle one, breaks it in two, wraps up the larger part, and sets it aside for the afikomen (the symbolic Seder dessert). The leader takes the smaller part, replaces it in the middle, and wraps them all in a sack. In the Sephardic tradition, each willing participant slings the sack over his or her shoulder.

ALL: "Mi attah?" - Who are you?
PARTICIPANT: "Ani Yehudi." - I am a Jew.
ALL: From where are you coming?
PARTICIPANT: From Egypt.
ALL: And where are you going?
PARTICIPANT: To Jerusalem.

The matzot are placed back on the Seder plate and the afikomen is hidden.

> Why do we hide the larger piece of matzah? Some say it is because more is hidden than revealed. We ask questions and seek out the hidden messages of this special holiday.

5. MAGGID - Telling the story

מַגִּיד

Matzah bag
Moravia, 1904

The leader lifts up a (fourth) piece of matzah.

LEADER:

This matzah is the "Matzah of Hope." We set it aside as a symbol of hope for those Jews throughout the world who are not free to celebrate Passover.

Each participant lifts up a piece of matzah.

ALL:

This is the bread of affliction which our
ancestors ate in the land of Egypt.
Let all those who are hungry come and
eat with us.
Let all those who are in need come and
share our meal.
This year we are here.
This year we are still slaves.
Next year may we all be free.

The matzot are covered. The second cup of wine is filled.

> Are there still people who are not free? In what ways are they still enslaved?

THE FOUR QUESTIONS

מַה נִּשְׁתַּנָּה הַלַּיְלָה הַזֶּה מִכָּל הַלֵּילוֹת: שֶׁבְּכָל הַלֵּילוֹת אָנוּ אוֹכְלִין חָמֵץ וּמַצָּה הַלַּיְלָה הַזֶּה כֻּלּוֹ מַצָּה: שֶׁבְּכָל הַלֵּילוֹת אָנוּ אוֹכְלִין שְׁאָר יְרָקוֹת הַלַּיְלָה הַזֶּה מָרוֹר. שֶׁבְּכָל הַלֵּילוֹת אֵין אָנוּ מַטְבִּילִין אֲפִילוּ פַּעַם אֶחָת, הַלַּיְלָה הַזֶּה שְׁתֵּי פְעָמִים. שֶׁבְּכָל הַלֵּילוֹת אָנוּ אוֹכְלִין בֵּין יוֹשְׁבִין וּבֵין מְסֻבִּין, הַלַּיְלָה הַזֶּה כֻּלָּנוּ מְסֻבִּין

From
The Haggadah
Arthur Szyk, 1965

"Ma Nishtana," (The Four Questions), is traditionally recited by the youngest child at the table.

MA NISH-TA-NAH HA-LAI-LAH HA-ZEH MI-KOL HA-LAI-LOT?
SHE-B'CHOL HA-LEY-LOT A-NU OCH'LEEN CHA-MAYTZ
U-MA-TZAH. HA-LAI-LAH HA-ZEH KU-LO MA-TZAH?

SHE-B'CHOL HA-LAY-LOT A-NU O-CH'LEEN SH'AR Y'RA-KOT.
HA-LAI-LAH HA-ZEH MA-ROR?

SHE-B'CHOL HA-LAY-LOT AYN A-NU MAT-BI-LIN A-FI-LU PA-AM
E-CHAT. HA-LAI-LAH HA-ZEH SH'TAY P'A-MIM?

SHE-B'CHOL HA-LAY-LOT A-NU O-CH'LEEN BAYN YOSH-VEEN
U-VAYN M'SU-BIN. HA-LAI-LAH HA-ZEH KU-LA-NU M'SU-BIN?

How does this night differ from all other nights? On all other nights we eat either leavened or unleavened bread. Why on this night do we eat only unleavened bread?

On all other nights we eat all kinds of herbs. Why on this night do we eat only bitter herbs?

On all other nights we need not dip our herbs even once. Why on this night do we need to dip twice?

On all other nights we eat sitting or reclining. Why on this night do we recline?

THE ANSWERS

The matzot are uncovered.

PARTICIPANT:

This night is different from all other nights because of our unique celebration of freedom. We eat only matzah to highlight the tale of our hasty exodus from Egypt.

We eat bitter herbs so that we too may sample at least a taste of bitterness.

We dip our bitter herbs twice, once in salt water and once in sweet charoset, as we remember both the salty tears of our ancestors and the sweetness of their hope for freedom.

As a symbol of our comfort, we recline and eat as free men and women.

From *Passover Haggadah* - Darmstadt, Germany, 1733

PARTICIPANT:

A tale is told about five rabbis on a Passover evening during the beginning of the second century of the Common Era. While reclining at a Seder, they told and retold the story of the Exodus from Egypt all through the night. One of their disciples came running to tell them, "It's time to read the morning Sh'ma, the time for morning prayers." These five sages, even though well versed in the story, had reviewed the story over and over again, suggesting that they wanted to savor every nuance of the narrative. This evening, we too are discovering new meanings as we retell this ancient story.

Avadim Hayinu

PARTICIPANT:

We were all slaves to Pharaoh in Egypt. And the Lord our God delivered us with a mighty hand and an outstretched arm. If God had not brought our ancestors out of Egypt, then we, our children, and our children's children would have remained slaves. So, even if all of us were scholars, full of understanding and wisdom, and learned in Torah, it would still be our obligation to tell the story of how we left Egypt. Everyone who studies the meaning of the Exodus from Egypt deserves praise.

This beautiful and ancient song is a remarkable, timeless allegory. We realize that Pharaohs are not the only oppressive leaders, Egypt is not the only place where people feel trapped and the Israelites are not the only ones seeking and struggling to obtain freedom. We celebrate and relive our Exodus not only to remember our enslavement, but also to highlight the manner in which we were freed. We are inspired to consider how we can protect and assure the freedom of all people.

From the *Barcelona Haggadah* - Barcelona, mid-14th century

Name all the things you see in this picture.

From *The Golden Haggadah* - Spain, probably Barcelona, c. 1320

THE FOUR CHILDREN (Pam's favorite part)

As you read the haggadah, identify *your* favorite part.

LEADER:

The Torah commands us four times to teach our children about the Exodus from Egypt. Rabbis have said there are four kinds of children, each of whom learns in a different way. Our challenge is to find the answers which best respond to each child's questions.

PARTICIPANT:

The **wise child** asks, "What is the meaning of the laws of Pesach?" This eager child has a thirst for knowledge and is told all that he or she may grasp in the experience of the Seder.

"The Four Sons" from *Song of David / The Moss Haggadah* David Moss, 1980

PARTICIPANT:

The **wicked child** asks, "What does this celebration mean to *you*?" This isolated child does not include himself or herself in the question and acts like a stranger at the Seder. We challenge this child's defiance by saying, "Had you been in Egypt at the time of the Exodus, you would not have been included when God freed our ancestors from slavery." The invitation to learn and participate in the Seder remains open, reflecting the belief that we all have the ability to change.

PARTICIPANT:

The **simple child** asks, "What is this all about?" We teach this unpretentious and impressionable child about the story of Exodus in terms that he or she may understand. We afford this child all the attention needed to grasp what is within his or her capacity.

PARTICIPANT:

There is a **child who does not know how to ask.** We entertain this young child with all that is in front of him. Let him grasp what he may and allow his imagination to flourish.

THE STORY

CHILD:

Many years ago, long before any of us was born, there was a wicked king named Pharaoh who ruled in the land of Egypt. Many Israelites lived there peacefully with the Egyptians. Pharaoh was afraid there were too many Israelites and that they were becoming too powerful. He commanded that they become slaves and forced them to build cities and palaces for him. Even Israelite children had to work for Pharaoh. Pharaoh and his men shouted:

From *The Haggadah of Passover* - Sigmund Forst, 1955

YOUNGEST CHILDREN:

BANG, BANG, BANG...
HOLD YOUR HAMMER LOW.
BANG, BANG, BANG...
GIVE A HEAVY BLOW.

FOR IT'S WORK, WORK, WORK...
EVERY DAY AND EVERY NIGHT.
FOR IT'S WORK, WORK, WORK...
WHEN IT'S DARK AND WHEN
IT'S LIGHT.

DIG, DIG, DIG...
GET YOUR SHOVEL DEEP.
DIG, DIG, DIG...
THERE'S NO TIME FOR SLEEP.

FOR IT'S WORK, WORK, WORK...
EVERY DAY AND EVERY NIGHT.
FOR IT'S WORK, WORK, WORK...
WHEN IT'S DARK AND WHEN
IT'S LIGHT.

Building Cities

CHILD:

King Pharaoh was mean to Israelite adults and children. Wicked King Pharaoh did not want Israelite children to grow to be adults. One Israelite mother was afraid and wanted to protect her child from Pharaoh and his men. She put her baby in a basket made of reeds and placed him by the river Nile. Pharaoh's daughter, the princess, was walking by the river bank and found the baby. She brought him to her palace and named him Moses, which means "pulled from the water." The princess knew Moses was an Israelite, but she kept it a secret, and raised him as a prince.

From *Haggadah of Passover* - Dr. Joseph Loewy & Joseph Guens - Tel Aviv, after 1945

CHILD:

As Moses grew to be a man, he found out that he was an Israelite and he saw how cruel King Pharaoh was. One day he saw an Egyptian beating a slave, became angry, and killed the Egyptian. Afraid for his life, Moses fled Egypt and became a shepherd in a faraway land.

Let My People Go - from "The Story of Exodus" series
Marc Chagall - Jerusalem, 1967

CHILD:

One day, while looking for a lost sheep, Moses saw a bush that was on fire but that was not burning up. From the bush came God's voice. The Voice told Moses to go back to Egypt to free the Children of Israel and take them far away. Moses returned to Egypt and went to see Pharaoh. Moses said to Pharaoh, "If you do not free the Children of Israel, you shall be punished." The wicked king did not believe Moses and said, "No." God was angry with Pharaoh and punished him and the Egyptians ten times. These punishments are called the ten plagues.

Let My People Go

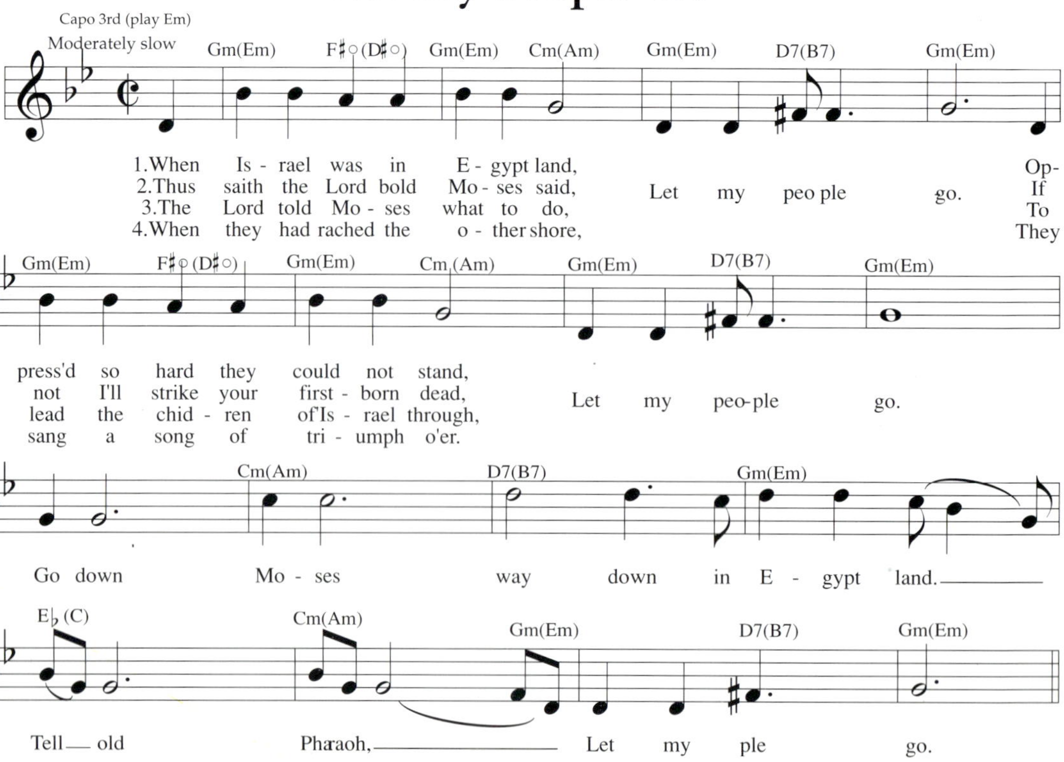

THE TEN PLAGUES

LEADER:

These are the plagues that God brought upon the Egyptians in Egypt. Now as we mention each plague, we will spill some wine. We must acknowledge that all people are God's creatures and that our joy is lessened when anyone, even our enemy, suffers.

דָּם

1. BLOOD

צְפַרְדֵּעַ

2. FROGS

כִּנִּים

3. LICE

עָרוֹב

4. BEASTS

דֶּבֶר

5. CATTLE BLIGHT

מַכַּת בְּכוֹרוֹת

10. SLAYING OF THE FIRST BORN

חֹשֶׁךְ

9. DARKNESS

אַרְבֶּה

8. LOCUSTS

בָּרָד

7. HAIL

שְׁחִין

6. BOILS

? Do we still have plagues? Can you give an example?

CHILDREN:

ONE MORNING, KING PHARAOH
WOKE UP IN HIS BED.
THERE WERE FROGS IN HIS BED
AND FROGS ON HIS HEAD.
FROGS ON HIS NOSE, AND FROGS
ON HIS TOES,
FROGS HERE, FROGS THERE,
FROGS WERE JUMPING EVERYWHERE!

CHILD:

At last, Pharaoh was frightened and let the Israelites go. They hurried out of Egypt, without time to bake bread for their journey. Instead, they put raw dough on their backs which the sun baked into hard crackers called matzot. The children of Israel followed Moses to the edge of the Red Sea and the sea divided.

CHILD:

The Israelites crossed safely on dry land to the other side. Pharaoh changed his mind and told his men to chase after them. When the Israelites were safely past the sea, the sea fell upon Pharaoh's men. Moses led the Israelites safely into the desert toward the Promised Land. Miriam, Moses' sister, led the Israelites in dance and song, as they celebrated their long-awaited freedom.

Passover Haggadah
Raphael Abecassis, 1993

As Pharaoh's men were engulfed by the Red Sea, Angels were singing praises to God. God silenced them saying, "My children perish. Cease your songs."

Child:

On their journey that would lead them to the Promised Land, the Children of Israel entered into a covenant with God at Mount Sinai and received the Commandments. They had many children, and their children had many children. Our Jewish parents and grandparents came from these families.

The 14th-century *Sarajevo Haggadah* accompanied the Jews expelled from Spain in 1492. It remained in Sarajevo with one family until the 19th century when they sold it to the National Museum. Hidden from the Nazis in a peasant hut, it later miraculously survived the Bosnian War when many other ancient manuscripts were destroyed.

From the *Sarajevo Haggadah* - Barcelona, 14th century

Leader:

According to the Mishnah (code of ancient Jewish law), Rabbi Gamliel said: "Whoever does not consider the meaning of these three, **PESACH, MATZAH, MAROR,** has not fulfilled the purpose of the Seder." (Pesahim 10.5)

The leader points to each symbol as it is mentioned.

All:

PESACH, a shankbone, is a reminder that God "passed over" the houses of our ancestors in Egypt during the tenth plague.

MATZAH is meant to recall our hasty flight from Egypt. We fulfill the mitzvah, "For seven days you eat matzah, that you may remember your departure from Egypt as long as you live." (Exodus 12.15)

MAROR, the bitter herb, is the symbol of the bitterness of servitude. May we have sympathy for all who are enslaved by virtue of their heredity, environment, or self-imposed limitations.

PARTICIPANT:

Let us take a moment to remember our brethren who have been enslaved at various times in history, and those who are still not free today. The following is a poem written by an 11-year-old boy while he was in Terezin concentration camp during World War II.

I AM A JEW

I am a Jew and will be a Jew forever.
Even if I should die from hunger,
  never will I submit.
I will always fight for my people,
  on my honor.
I will never be ashamed of them,
I give my word.
I am proud of my people,
how dignified they are.
Even though I am suppressed,
I will always come back to life.

Franta Bass
(from *I Never Saw Another Butterfly*,
edited by Hana Volavkova, 1993.
Schocken Books, Inc., New York)

From the *Birds' Head Haggadah* - Southern Germany, c. 1300

During the Holocaust, Jews still celebrated Passover, but often had to eat bread, as matzah was unavailable. The Jews in the Warsaw Ghetto said a special prayer: "Our prayer to You is that You may keep us alive and save us and rescue us speedily so that we may observe Your commandments and do Your will and serve You with a perfect heart." Amen.

ALL:

We recall God's second promise, " I will deliver you from their bondage."

בָּרוּךְ אַתָּה יְיָ אֱלֹהֵינוּ מֶלֶךְ הָעוֹלָם בּוֹרֵא פְּרִי הַגָּפֶן.

Ba-ruch a-tah A-do-nai E-lo-hey-nu me-lech ha-o-lam bo-rey p'ri ha-ga-fen.

Blessed are You, Eternal God, Ruler of the Universe, who creates the fruit of the vine.

All drink the second cup of wine.

DAYENU

PARTICIPANT:

Dayenu means, "It would have been enough for us." The meaning of this hymn is that any one of the things God did for us, as mentioned in each verse, would have been enough to deserve our gratitude.

אִלּוּ הוֹצִיאָנוּ מִמִּצְרַיִם - דַּיֵּנוּ
I-LU HO-TZI-ANU MI-MITZ'RA-YIM -- DAYENU
Had God only taken us out of Egypt - DAYENU

אִלּוּ נָתַן לָנוּ אֶת הַשַּׁבָּת - דַּיֵּנוּ
I-LU NA-TAN LA-NU ET HA-SHABBAT -- DAYENU
Had God only given us Shabbat - DAYENU

אִלּוּ נָתַן לָנוּ אֶת הַתּוֹרָה - דַּיֵּנוּ
I-LU NA-TAN LA-NU ET HA-TO-RAH -- DAYENU
Had God only given us the Torah - DAYENU

אִלּוּ הִכְנִיסָנוּ לְאֶרֶץ יִשְׂרָאֵל - דַּיֵּנוּ
I-LU HICH'NIY-SA-NU L'E-RETZ YIS-RA-EL -- DAYENU
Had God only brought us to the Land of Israel - DAYENU

6. RACHTZAH - Second hand washing
רָחְצָה

LEADER:

We wash our hands in preparation for eating the matzah. This time we say a blessing.

בָּרוּךְ אַתָּה יְיָ אֱלֹהֵינוּ מֶלֶךְ הָעוֹלָם אֲשֶׁר קִדְּשָׁנוּ בְּמִצְוֹתָיו וְצִוָּנוּ עַל נְטִילַת יָדָיִם.

Ba-ruch a-tah A-do-nai E-lo-hey-nu me-lech ha-o-lam a-sher kid'sha-nu b'mitz-vo-tav v'tzi-va-nu al n'ti-lat ya-da-yim.

Blessed are You, Eternal God, Ruler of the Universe, who has sanctified us with laws and commanded us to wash our hands.

The leader and others wash their hands.

7. MOTZI MATZAH - Blessing for the matzah
מוֹצִיא מַצָּה

The leader lifts the three matzot.

ALL:

בָּרוּךְ אַתָּה יְיָ אֱלֹהֵינוּ מֶלֶךְ הָעוֹלָם הַמּוֹצִיא לֶחֶם מִן הָאָרֶץ.

Ba-ruch a-tah A-do-nai E-lo-hey-nu me-lech ha-o-lam ha-mo-tzi le-chem min ha-a-retz.

Blessed are You, Eternal God, Ruler of the Universe, who brings bread from the earth.

Matzah cover
Jerusalem, early 20th century

ALL:

בָּרוּךְ אַתָּה יְיָ אֱלֹהֵינוּ מֶלֶךְ הָעוֹלָם אֲשֶׁר קִדְּשָׁנוּ
בְּמִצְוֹתָיו וְצִוָּנוּ עַל אֲכִילַת מַצָּה.

Ba-ruch a-tah A-do-nai E-lo-hey-nu me-lech ha-o-lam a-sher kid'sha-nu
b'mitz-vo-tav v'tzi-va-nu al a-chi-lat ma-tzah.

Blessed are You, Lord our God, Ruler of the Universe, who has sanctified
us with laws and commanded us to eat matzah.

The bottom matzah is put back in its place. The top and middle matzot are distributed. All eat matzah while reclining.

SOMEONE WHO DOESN'T LIKE MATZAH RECITES:

This is the poorest, the driest of bread.
It crinkles and crumbles all over our beds.
This is the matzah that Grand-Daddy ate
When he zoomed out of Egypt, afraid he'd belate.
You're welcome to join us--Come one or come many!
I'll give you my matzah. I sure don't want any.

From *Uncle Eli's Haggadah*
Eliezer Segal, 1998
No Starch Press, San Francisco

HANG IN, FOOD SOON!

8. MAROR - The bitter herbs
מָרוֹר

PARTICIPANT:

Let us each dip a piece of maror into charoset as we recall the bitterness of slavery. We recite the blessing.

בָּרוּךְ אַתָּה יְיָ אֱלֹהֵינוּ מֶלֶךְ הָעוֹלָם אֲשֶׁר קִדְּשָׁנוּ
בְּמִצְוֹתָיו וְצִוָּנוּ עַל אֲכִילַת מָרוֹר.

Ba-ruch a-tah A-do-nai E-lo-hey-nu me-lech ha-o-lam a-sher kid'sha-nu b'mitz-vo-tav v'tzi-va-nu al a-chi-lat ma-ror.

Blessed are You, Eternal God, Ruler of the Universe, who has sanctified us with laws and commanded us to eat bitter herbs.

All dip the bitter herbs in charoset and eat while reclining.

According to a midrash (rabbinic commentary), enslaved Israelites called Pharaoh "Maror" because he embittered their lives.

Making Haroset - Toby Knobel Fluek, Czernica, Poland, 1975

9. KORECH - Hillel's sandwich
כּוֹרֵךְ

PARTICIPANT:

When the Temple still stood, Hillel would make a sandwich of matzah and maror and eat them together with charoset. The charoset reminds us of the cement used to glue the bricks together when we built Pharaoh's cities.

The bottom matzah is distributed for Hillel's sandwich. Take a piece of matzah and break it into 2 pieces. Add the chazeret, the second kind of bitter herb, as the middle of the sandwich, dip the sandwich into charoset, and eat it while reclining . . . in one mouthful if you dare.

THE SHANKBONE (Zeroah)

In the Sephardic tradition, pieces of meat from the shankbone are eaten by each participant. In the Ashkenazi tradition, the shankbone is acknowledged but not eaten.

PARTICIPANT:

The "shank" is the limb of an animal. We remember that God saved us "with an outstretched arm."

THE EGG (Beitza)

It is customary to start off our meal with an egg flavored with salt or salt water.

PARTICIPANT:

We remember the new life the Children of Israel made for themselves when they left slavery so long ago.

First Seder in Jerusalem - Reuven Rubin, Tel Aviv, 1950

10. SHULCHAN ORECH - The meal
שֻׁלְחָן עוֹרֵךְ

LEADER:

Shulchan orech means "the set table." This is when the famous Seder question "When do we eat?" can be answered,

"Now!"

The Seder plate is removed from the table.
When the meal is finished, children search for the afikomen.

Passover Seders

Conducted By

JAN PEERCE

DEAUVILLE HOTEL

Napoleon Room

First Seder — April 2, 1969
7:00 P.M.

Second Seder — April 3, 1969
7:00 P.M.

Menu

Traditional Bitter Herbs — Sacramental Wine

Charoses, Hard Boiled Egg, Salt Water

Crisp Celery Hearts — Rosebud Radishes

Stuffed Fresh Water Fish, Beet Horseradish

Chicken Broth with Matzoh Ball

ROAST HALF SPRING CHICKEN
Deauville Dressing

Potato Kugel — Carrot Tzimmes

Tossed Green Salad
French Dressing

Honey Cake
Lemon Sponge Cake — Passover Macaroons

Cafe Noir — Orange Pekoe Tea

Passover Seder menu - Well-known Jewish musicians often appeared at hotel Seders. Jan Peerce (1904-1984), a Metropolitan Opera star, conducted the Seder at the Deauville Hotel in Miami Beach, 1969.

11. TZAFUN - The afikomen
צָפוּן

The Seder plate is returned to the table.

Leader:

Tzafun means "hidden." Afikomen means "dessert." Since tradition tells us that neither the meal nor the Seder can be concluded without finding and eating the hidden dessert, whoever finds it may demand a reward.

Children -- Now is the time for you to negotiate your reward.
Parents and grandparents -- **We need you!**

All eat the afikomen. The third cup of wine is filled.

Pouch for afikomen
China, 19th century

12. BARECH - Blessing after the meal
בָּרֵךְ

LEADER:

It is a mitzvah to say grace after meals. As it is written, "When you have eaten and are satisfied, you shall bless the Lord, your God, for the good land which God has given you."

ALL: Praised are You, Adonai our God, Ruler of the Universe, who in goodness, mercy, and kindness gives food to the world.

Blessed is our God whose food we have eaten and by whose goodness we live.

Praised are You, Adonai, our God, who provides food for all life.

Blessed be Your Name forever in the mouth of every living thing.

Praised be the Creator of Life.

Seder show towel
Alsace, France, 1821

בִּרְכַּת הַמָּזוֹן (Grace)

LEADER: רַבּוֹתַי נְבָרֵךְ:
ALL: יְהִי שֵׁם יְיָ מְבֹרָךְ מֵעַתָּה וְעַד עוֹלָם:
LEADER: בִּרְשׁוּת מָרָנָן וְרַבָּנָן וְרַבּוֹתַי, נְבָרֵךְ אֱלֹהֵינוּ שֶׁאָכַלְנוּ מִשֶּׁלּוֹ.
ALL: בָּרוּךְ אֱלֹהֵינוּ שֶׁאָכַלְנוּ מִשֶּׁלּוֹ וּבְטוּבוֹ חָיִינוּ:

בָּרוּךְ אַתָּה יְיָ אֱלֹהֵינוּ מֶלֶךְ הָעוֹלָם הַזָּן אֶת הָעוֹלָם כֻּלּוֹ
בְּטוּבוֹ, בְּחֵן בְּחֶסֶד וּבְרַחֲמִים: הוּא נוֹתֵן לֶחֶם לְכָל בָּשָׂר, כִּי
לְעוֹלָם חַסְדּוֹ: וּבְטוּבוֹ הַגָּדוֹל תָּמִיד לֹא חָסַר לָנוּ, וְאַל יֶחְסַר
לָנוּ מָזוֹן לְעוֹלָם וָעֶד: בַּעֲבוּר שְׁמוֹ הַגָּדוֹל. כִּי הוּא זָן וּמְפַרְנֵס
לַכֹּל, וּמֵטִיב לַכֹּל, וּמֵכִין מָזוֹן לְכָל בְּרִיּוֹתָיו אֲשֶׁר בָּרָא:
בָּרוּךְ אַתָּה יְיָ, הַזָּן אֶת הַכֹּל.
כַּכָּתוּב וְאָכַלְתָּ וְשָׂבָעְתָּ וּבֵרַכְתָּ אֶת־יְיָ אֱלֹהֶיךָ עַל־הָאָרֶץ
הַטֹּבָה אֲשֶׁר נָתַן־לָךְ: בָּרוּךְ אַתָּה יְיָ עַל־הָאָרֶץ וְעַל־הַמָּזוֹן.
וּבְנֵה יְרוּשָׁלַיִם עִיר הַקֹּדֶשׁ בִּמְהֵרָה בְיָמֵינוּ.
בָּרוּךְ אַתָּה יְיָ בּוֹנֵה בְרַחֲמָיו יְרוּשָׁלָיִם. אָמֵן.
עֹשֶׂה שָׁלוֹם בִּמְרוֹמָיו הוּא יַעֲשֶׂה שָׁלוֹם עָלֵינוּ וְעַל כָּל יִשְׂרָאֵל,
וְאִמְרוּ אָמֵן.

ALL:

We recall the third divine promise, "I will redeem you with an outstretched arm."

בָּרוּךְ אַתָּה יְיָ אֱלֹהֵינוּ מֶלֶךְ הָעוֹלָם בּוֹרֵא פְּרִי הַגָּפֶן.

Ba-ruch a-tah A-do-nai E-lo-hey-nu me-lech ha-o-lam bo-rey p'ri ha-ga-fen.

Blessed are You, Eternal God, Ruler of the Universe, who creates the fruit of the vine.

All drink the third cup of wine.

ELIYAHU

Kiddush cup
Palestine, 20th century

ANY CHILD STILL AT THE TABLE :

There is an extra cup of wine at the table. This is the cup for Eliyahu. There is a tale that Eliyahu, or Elijah, a great teacher who lived many years ago, visits every Seder to wish everyone a year of peace and freedom. As we open the door for Elijah, we recognize that Passover is a night for openness. We open our doors to visitors, our minds to learning and personal growth, and our hearts to those less fortunate.

> One tradition is to begin with Elijah's cup empty. Before opening the door, pass the cup around, allowing everyone to pour a little wine from each of their cups to fill Elijah's cup. This reminds us that we must all do our parts to make this a better world and assure our redemption.

The door is opened. Elijah's filled cup remains on the table.

ALL SING:

אֵלִיָּהוּ הַנָּבִיא, אֵלִיָּהוּ הַתִּשְׁבִּי, אֵלִיָּהוּ, אֵלִיָּהוּ, אֵלִיָּהוּ הַגִּלְעָדִי,
בִּמְהֵרָה בְיָמֵינוּ יָבֹא אֵלֵינוּ, עִם מָשִׁיחַ בֶּן דָּוִד, עִם מָשִׁיחַ בֶּן דָּוִד.

Eliyahu Hanavi

Watch Eliyahu's cup to see if any of the wine disappears.

The door is closed.

From the *Second Cincinnati Haggadah* - Amsterdam, 1716/17

13. HALLEL - Praising God
הַלֵּל

> Many parts of the Seder are structured in 4's. How many can you name?

The 4th cup of wine is filled.

PARTICIPANT:

It is our duty to thank and praise, laud and glorify, extol and honor, exalt and adore God who performed all these miracles for our fathers and mothers and for us.

May it be Your will to bring all families who are suffering persecution into freedom as You brought our ancestors to freedom.

May we be worthy to enjoy the Passover holiday together with all the families of Israel in freedom and unity.

Amen.

14. NIRTZAH - Conclusion
נִרְצָה

PARTICIPANT:

As our Seder draws to a close, we raise our cups of wine. The final cup recalls us to our covenant with the Eternal One, reminds us that tasks still await us as a people, and validates a great purpose for which the people of Israel live: the preservation and affirmation of hope.

ALL:

As it is written, "And I will take you to be my people."

בָּרוּךְ אַתָּה יְיָ אֱלֹהֵינוּ מֶלֶךְ הָעוֹלָם בּוֹרֵא פְּרִי הַגָּפֶן.

Ba-ruch a-tah A-do-nai E-lo-hey-nu me-lech ha-o-lam bo-rey p'ri ha-ga-fen.

Blessed are You, Eternal God, Ruler of the Universe, who creates the fruit of the vine.

All drink the 4th cup of wine.

Israel Independence Day celebration, 1948

From the film *The Animated Haggadah* - Rony Oren, 1985

Many feel this ancient Aramaic song is best sung faster and faster with each verse.

Chad Gadya

ONE LITTLE GOAT

There was one little goat. One very little goat that my father bought for two zuzim...
One little goat, One very little goat.

Then came a cat and ate the goat that my father bought for two zuzim...
One little goat, One very little goat.

Then came a dog and bit the cat that ate the goat that my father bought for two zuzim...
One little goat, One very little goat.

Then came a stick and beat the dog that bit the cat that ate the goat that my father bought for two zuzim...
One little goat, One very little goat.

Then came a fire and burned the stick that beat the dog that bit the cat that ate the goat that my father bought for two zuzim...
One little goat, One very little goat.

From *Haggadah* - Hamburg, 1740/41

Then came the water and quenched the fire that burned the stick that beat the dog that bit the cat that ate the goat that my father bought for two zuzim...
One little goat, One very little goat.

Then came the ox and drank the water that quenched the fire that burned the stick that beat the dog that bit the cat that ate the goat that my father bought for two zuzim...
One little goat, One very little goat.

Then came the slaughterer and slaughtered the ox that drank the water that quenched the fire that burned the stick that beat the dog that bit the cat that ate the goat that my father bought for two zuzim...
One little goat, One very little goat.

Then came the angel of death and killed the slaughterer who slaughtered the ox that drank the water that quenched the fire that burned the stick that beat the dog that bit the cat that ate the goat that my father bought for two zuzim...
One little goat, One very little goat.

Then came God, blessed be His name, and He slew the angel of death who killed the slaughterer who slaughtered the ox that drank the water that quenched the fire that burned the stick that beat the dog that bit the cat that ate the goat that my father bought for two zuzim...
One little goat, One very little goat.

("Chad Gadya" - Aramaic - continued)

(verse)

4th. V'a-tah nu-rah v'sa-raf l'chu-trah
d'hi-kah l'chal-bah d'na-shach
l'shun-rah d'a-chal l'gad-ya di-z'van
a-bah bit-rei zu-zei...
Chad gad-ya, chad gad-ya.

5th. V'a-tah ma-yah v'cha-vah l'nu-rah
d'sa-raf l'chu-trah d'hi-kah
l'chal-bah d'na-shach
l'shun-rah d'a-chal l'gad-ya
di-z'van a-bah bit-rei zu-zei...
Chad gad-ya, chad gad-ya.

6th. V'a-tah to-rah v'sha-tah
l'ma-yah d'cha-vah l'nu-rah
d'sa-raf l'chu-trah d'hi-kah
l'chal-bah d'na-shach
l'shun-rah d'a-chal l'gad-ya
di-z'van a-bah bit-rei zu-zei...
Chad gad-ya, chad gad-ya.

7th. V'a-tah ha-sho-cheit v'sha-chat l'to-rah
d'sha-tah l'ma-yah d'cha-vah l'nu-rah
d'sa-raf l'chu-trah d'hi-kah l'chal-bah
d'na-shach l'shun-rah d'a-chal l'gad-ya
di-z'van a-bah bit-rei zu-zei...
Chad gad-ya, chad gad-ya.

8th. V'a-tah mal-ach ha-ma-vet v'sha-chat
la-sho-cheit d'sha-chat l'to-rah d'sha-tah
l'ma-yah d'cha-vah l'nu-rah, d'sa-raf
l'chu-trah d'hi-kah l'chal-bah d'na-shach
l'shun-rah d'a-chal l'gad-ya di-z'van
a-bah bit-rei zu-zei...
Chad gad-ya, chad gad-ya.

9th. V'a-tah Ha-ka-dosh ba-ruch Hu
v'sha-chat l'mal-ach ha-ma-vet
d'sha-chat la-sho-cheit d'sha-chat l'to-rah
d'sha-tah l'ma-yah d'cha-vah l'nu-rah
d'sa-raf l'chu-trah d'hi-kah l'chal-bah
d'na-shach l'shun-rah d'a-chal l'gad-ya
di-z'van a-bah bit-rei zu-zei...
Chad gad-ya, chad gad-ya.

SOURCES

Cover. *The Seder*
Meichel Pressman, 1950.
Watercolor on paper, 12.2"x18.5".
The Jewish Museum, New York.

(indexed by page number)

ii. *Second Cincinnati Haggadah*
Amsterdam, 1716/17.
Hebrew Union College (HUC) - Jewish Institute of Religion, Klau Library, Cincinnati.
This extraordinary haggadah includes oil miniatures on parchment inspired by engravings found in the printed *Amsterdam Haggadah* of 1712.

1. *Spanish Haggadah*
Spain, 1350-1360.
British Library, London.
The "Ha Lachma Anya" ceremony shows the father placing a basket of Matzot on the head of a child. It was then placed successively on the heads of each participant. The illuminations in this haggadah, typical of Sephardic haggadot, emphasized ceremonial rites of the holiday.

2. *Haggadah for Passover*
Hebrew Publishing Co., New York, 1921.
This Seder scene is the first illustration in this popular Hebrew and English haggadah. Note the leader's cushion, wine, candles and the pitcher of water being carried to the table for "Urchatz."

5. Tiered Seder Plate
Vienna, 1814.
Silver, cast, pierced, and engraved, 14.75"x16".
Franz Strobl (?), active 1811-1843.
Hebrew Union College (HUC) Skirball Cultural Center and Museum, Los Angeles.
This Seder plate includes three tiers for matzot. Such tiering was a signature feature of plates in 19th-century Europe. The central figure is Elijah.

6. Kiddush cup from *The Haggadah*
Arthur Szyk, 1965.
"Massadah" and "Alumoth," Jerusalem and Tel Aviv.
Reprinted with the permission of The Arthur Szyk Society and Alexandra Bracie. (1200 Edgehill Dr., Burlingame, CA 94010).
This modern illuminated haggadah was termed "the most beautiful book ever published by human hands" by the *London Times*. 250 copies on vellum were produced in its first release in 1939. The haggadah was popularized in a velvet-covered edition in the 1960s.

7. *First Cincinnati Haggadah*
Southern Germany, c. 1480-90.
HUC - Jewish Institute of Religion, Klau Library, Cincinnati.
This typical Ashkenazi illuminated manuscript has illustrations in the margins including both biblical scenes and holiday rites. This marginal image, seen close up, is of a seated Rabbi Eliezer ben Azariah.

8. Matzah comb
Germany, 18th-19th century.
Iron, 8.75"x17.5".
The baking of matzah was and is carefully supervised so that the dough does not rise. To hasten baking and prevent rising, the surface is pierced by the spikes of a matzah roller or "comb."

8. Matzah bag
Moravia, 1904.
Jewish Museum, Mikulov (Nikolsburg), Moravia.
Velvet, embroidered with cotton, cotton and metallic fringe, cotton cord, linen damask lining, 17.5"x12.5".
A sectional bag with three compartments was in common use in Ashkenazi communities in Europe in the early 1900s. The embroidery included names for the symbols of the holiday and ceremonies of the Seder.

9. *The Haggadah*
Arthur Szyk, 1965.
"Massadah" and "Alumoth," Jerusalem and Tel Aviv.
Reprinted with the permission of The Arthur Szyk Society and Alexandra Bracie.
This magnificent "Ma Nishtana" depicts the talent and genius of the calligrapher/artist. In the spirit of his medieval predecessors, Szyk beautifully integrated calligraphy, narrative, illumination, and illustration to lead a modern resurgence of manuscript illumination.

10. *Passover Haggadah*
Darmstadt, Germany, 1733.
From facsimile, W. Turnowsky Ltd., Tel Aviv.
Original: Jewish National and University Library, Jerusalem.
The artist and scribe, Joseph ben David Aharon of Leipnik, painted in rich, warm colors. Illustrations were copied from well-known printed haggadot from Prague (1526), Mantua (1560), Venice (1601), and Amsterdam (1695). Costumes, backgrounds, and some detail were altered to suit the 18th-century German style. This manuscript is typical of those commissioned by wealthy Jews for themselves or in honor of their loved ones.

11. *Barcelona Haggadah*
Barcelona, mid-14thcentury.
The *Barcelona* is of the type of Spanish haggadah with full-sized illustrations within the text, as compared to *The Golden Haggadah* which has miniature illustrations. Illustrations are biblical, ritual, or textual as in this rendition of "Avadim Hayinu."

12. *The Golden Haggadah*
Spain, probably Barcelona, c. 1320.
British Library, London.
The Golden Haggadah is one of seventeen ancient haggadot found in Spain. Full-page miniatures, in ink and gold leaf on vellum, present biblical scenes of Genesis and Exodus: *Top Lt.* - Aaron greets Moses and his wife, Tzipporah; *Top Rt.* - Angel of the burning bush, Moses with shoes on and off; *Bot. Lt.* - Moses and Aaron speak before Pharaoh and two counselors; *Bot. Rt.* - Aaron holds the snake while Moses announces the miracle to gathering Jews.

13. "The Four Sons" from *Song of David / The Moss Haggadah*
David Moss, 1980.
Courtesy of: Bet Alpha Editions, PO Box 12711, Berkeley, CA 94712.
David Moss was commissioned in 1980 by Richard and Beatrice Levy to create a handwritten, illuminated haggadah for their personal collection. These four images are but a few of many remarkable acrylic paintings intermingled with the unique calligraphy of this exemplary modern haggadah.

14. *The Haggadah of Passover*
Sigmund Forst, 1955.
Shulsinger Bros. Linotyping & Publishing Co., New York.
Illustrated haggadot in the 1950s often depicted artists' renditions of biblical scenes. The colors and images are striking and memorable.

15. *Haggadah of Passover*
Dr. Joseph Loewy and Joseph Guens, after 1945.
Sinai Publishing, Tel Aviv.
Post-World War II illustrated haggadot included black & white and colorized etchings and paintings depicting midrashic interpretations of Bible stories. In addition to traditional text, this issue has detailed commentary, ritual instructions, and even musical scores. The cover includes a copper insert of an Israel scene.

16. *Haggadah of Passover*
Illustrations by Marc Chagall, 1987.
Leon Amiel Publisher, New York and Paris.
The Chagall haggadah paintings, originally commissioned more than 25 years prior to the publication of the haggadah, include the world famous "Story of Exodus" illustrated series.

19. "Parting of the Red Sea" from *Passover Haggadah*
Raphael Abecassis, 1993.
Razim Art, Netanya, Israel.
Raphael Abecassis's unique Passover paintings were photographed by Nissim Lev and intermingled with his beautifully transcribed text. This well-known and prolific Moroccan artist has produced four distinct haggadot, each with a slightly different emphasis and style.

20. *Sarajevo Haggadah*
Barcelona, 14th century.
The *Sarajevo Haggadah* is perhaps the best-known Hebrew illuminated manuscript. Full-page miniatures illustrate Bible stories from Creation through Moses blessing the Israelites. This haggadah, originally of Spanish origin, made its way to Italy in 1492 and eventually to the National Museum in Sarajevo.The Nazis tried to confiscate the well-known book, but the manuscript was hidden away by the director of the museum.

21. *Birds' Head Haggadah*
Southern Germany, c. 1300.
The *Birds' Head* is the oldest extant German illuminated haggadah. The figures are dressed in medieval German-Jewish garb, including the infamous "Jew's Hat" the Jews were forced to wear by the Church. The heads of Jews are replaced by those of birds to avoid any chance that a figure might be taken as a graven image. Other distortions such as blank faces or heads covered by helmets were also used.

23. Matzah cover
Jerusalem, early 20th century.
Velvet, silk & metallic embroidery, shells, sequins, fish scales.
HUC Skirball Cultural Center and Museum, Los Angeles.

24. *Making Haroset*
Toby Knobel Fluek, 1975.
Oil on canvas, 16"x20".
The painting presents the ingredients and tools needed to make charoset. Fluek, a Czernica resident, fled the city during the time of occupation and deportation during World War II and hid for the duration of the war.

25. *First Seder in Jerusalem*
Reuven Rubin, 1950.
Oil on canvas, 10.5"x64".
Reuven Rubin Museum, Tel Aviv.
Rubin was born in Romania and emigrated to Palestine in 1955. This colorful painting of a Seder scene depicts the walls of the Old City in the background with figures around the table representing varied Jewish communities or regions. All share in the hope for a peaceful future.

26. Seder menu from *American Heritage Haggadah*
Edited by D. Geffen, 1992.
Geffen Publishing House, Jerusalem and New York.

26. Pouch for afikomen
China, 19th century.
Cotton, satin, embroidery thread, gold thread, diam 5.75".
HUC Skirball Cultural Center and Museum, Los Angeles.
This small yet colorful pouch held the piece of matzah for the afikomen.

27. Seder show towel
Alsace, France, 1821.
Linen, embroidered with silk thread and silk ribbon, 50"x15.5".
HUC Skirball Cultural Center and Museum, Los Angeles, gift of Rabbi Folkman.
This embroidered towel was placed by the door in Alsatian homes to cover soiled towels used for the Seder handwashing. The towels were known as Sederwehl in the Judeo-Alsatian dialect.

28. Kiddush cup
Palestine, 20th century.
Ceramic, h 3.75", d 2.6".
HUC Skirball Cultural Center and Museum, Los Angeles.

29. *Second Cincinnati Haggadah*
Amsterdam, 1716/17.
HUC - Jewish Institute of Religion, Klau Library, Cincinnati.
The scribe was Wolf Loeb of Trebitsch. This elegant Seder scene is of a wealthy Jewish household in Amsterdam around 1700.

30. Photograph from *Israel*
Editors: A.B. Harman and Yigael Yadin, 1958.
Massadah Publishing Co., Tel Aviv and Jerusalem.
This colorful photo was taken on Independence Day, 1948.

31. *The Animated Haggadah*
Rony Oren, 1985.
Scopus Films, Woodhaven, New York.
This "Chad Gadya" scene is a photo of a creation in clay, modeled by Rony Oren for the delightful children's film, *The Animated Haggadah.*

32. *Haggadah*
Hamburg, 1740/41.
HUC - Jewish Institute of Religion, Klau Library, Cincinnati.
The *Hamburg's* oil miniatures follow illustrations from the 1712 *Amsterdam Haggadah*, but utilize a folk-art style found in other 18th-century haggadot. This miniature goat scene accompanies the traditional Aramaic song, "Chad Gadya."

(Every attempt was made to reach all publishers and artists.)

Contemporary photographs and drawings by Elie M. Gindi.

We are delighted that you have shared tonight's Seder v
below. Write down your favorite part or picture or leav
names and notes from the people who have used this hag

DATE	NAME	COMMENTS